THE CHARGE TO THE CHURCH

Stephen Kaung

ISBN: 978-1-942521-64-8

Available from:

Christian Testimony Ministry
4424 Huguenot Road
Richmond, Virginia 23235

www.christiantestimonyministry.com

Printed in USA

CONTENTS

PREFACE

Stephen Kaung gave these messages on vision in March and April of 2014 in Richmond, VA. This was not only a charge given to the assembly in Richmond, VA but to the body of Christ. Just as Paul's letters were to specific churches and people, yet the body of Christ has been enriched from them throughout the church age.

Without vision the people cast off restraint and each does what is right in his own eyes. When the church loses its vision, compromise and complacency come in and the building work ceases.

What is the vision that unites God's people? It is Christ and Him alone. And the purpose of the church is to bear this testimony of the Lord Jesus. May the message of this book turn the hearts of God's people back to Christ.

WHAT IS OUR CHARGE?

I Timothy 1:18—This charge, [my] child Timotheus, I commit to thee, according to the prophecies as to thee preceding, in order that thou mightest war by them the good warfare.

Let's have a word of prayer:

> *Dear Lord, as we continue in Thy presence, we want to remove our shoes because we are Thy bondservants. Lord, what dost Thou have to say to us? Speak, Thy servants heareth. In Thy name we pray. Amen.*

Brothers and sisters, I would like to do something different in this time we have together. I am not going to preach; I want to have a heart-to-heart talk with you. My heart is open to you, but whether your hearts are open, only God knows. But I do feel it is time that we really have a heart-to-heart talk.

PAUL'S CHARGE TO TIMOTHY

About two weeks ago as I was meditating before the Lord, the word *charge* came to me. We know that after Paul was released from his Roman imprisonment, he travelled around to revisit the places where he had labored before; but he also wanted to cover some new areas. In a sense, he was in a hurry to leave, so he left Timothy behind in Ephesus because the work there was not finished. Therefore, he gave this charge to Timothy, and this word *charge* impressed my heart.

GOD'S CHARGE TO ADAM AND EVE

When God created man, He gave him a charge. Even though He had provided everything for them in the garden of Eden, yet He did not want man to remain idle. In Genesis 2:18 we discover that God's charge to man was to till and to guard the garden. They were to till the ground to make it more productive. And they were to guard the garden because it had no wall and there was an enemy outside. God committed this duty to till and to guard to man, but unfortunately, man failed to keep the charge of God.

GOD'S CHARGE TO ABRAHAM

God also called Abraham and gave him a charge. This is recorded in Acts 7:2-3 and again in Genesis 12:1. God charged him to leave his native land and his kindred and go to the place where God would lead him. In carrying out that charge, we know the history of how there were ups and downs in the life of Abraham until finally he kept the charge of God.

GOD'S CHARGE TO THE NATION OF ISRAEL

Then we also remember how the children of Israel were in the land of captivity in Egypt. But God sent Moses to lead them out of captivity and bring them into the Promised Land, a land flowing with milk and honey. The charge was given and we know the story.

GOD'S RESTATING
OF THE CHARGE TO ISRAEL

After Moses led the children of Israel through thirty-eight years of wandering, they came back to the east side of the border of Canaan. There Moses gave them the book of Deuteronomy. It was a restating of the charge that had been given to them because the first generation of the children of Israel had come to the border of the Promised Land, but they failed to go in. Now they were at the border of Canaan again, and Moses encouraged them to go in and possess their possession.

Now what made me think of these things? It is because of the forty years mentioned in Moses' life. Forty years ago is when we first began in Richmond. So I would like to share with you some of the past history in order that we may really be before the Lord and consider the charge that God has given us.

THE PAST HISTORY OF
THE RICHMOND ASSEMBLY

There was a conference in the sixties called Wabanna. It was called the Wabanna conference because of its proximity to three cities—Washington DC, Baltimore and Annapolis. This conference began with a thought from brother Chase whom I knew very well but is now with the Lord. He was thinking of bringing people together—those who knew T. Austin-Sparks, Devern Fromke, and me, and that was the beginning of the Wabanna conference. Every summer there was such a conference with Brother Sparks, Brother Fromke and myself as the speakers. The conference place was not a very good one, but the spirit was good.

5

During one of the Wabanna conferences two sisters came from Richmond who were active in the charismatic movement which began in the sixties. When they came to the Wabanna conference, they heard something they had never heard before. Not only were they challenged by the Lord, they were also changed.

When they returned to Richmond, one of the sisters invited brother Chase to come for a visit. It was through brother Chase that I was introduced to this sister. So it was forty years ago that she invited me to come to her home for a weekend. Those who attended were mainly sisters with only two brothers—one was her husband and the other was a friend. So I visited this home occasionally. Then she asked if I could come once a month which I did. Again, they were mostly sisters, but gradually some young brothers heard of it and began to come. Some of those young brothers are here now, but not young anymore.

When the Wabanna Conference came to an end in 1973, I asked the little group that was meeting in the sister's home whether we should have a small conference in Richmond. We all felt good about it, and in 1973 we had the first conference. The first two conferences were for adults, but after that it became a family conference. That first conference was held in the Episcopalian Diocese Center on River Road. It could only accommodate seventy people but we had about one hundred. Devern Fromke and I were the speakers. Then we had the second conference in 1974 and Lance Lambert of England was invited to come.

After that second conference I asked this small group of brothers and sisters whether there was the need for the testimony of Jesus in the city of Richmond. I did not mean that there were no churches in Richmond. On the contrary, we find that Richmond is a city of churches. Nor did I mean that there were no Christians; there were many Christians around. But was there a testimony of Jesus, a corporate testimony, an expression of that testimony? That is something God had revealed to us. Finally, we decided to pray about it. After prayer, we felt God's need of it. But instead of remaining in the sister's home, we felt the gathering should come out of her home and that the brothers should be in responsibility. There were three sisters at that time who were in responsibility. They were so gracious. They were willing to step back and support the young brothers. That is how the assembly began in 1974. We did not have a place of our own, so we moved to different places until, finally, the Lord located us in this place on Huguenot Road.

Because we felt there was a charge upon us, therefore we met together for that purpose. The Lord began to increase the number of brethren, and not only that, in the eighties in this country there were other places that had the same burden for the testimony of Jesus. I think it was 1995 that we came together and went through some of the subjects such as "Who Are We?", "Why Do we So Gather", and so forth.

THE ENEMY ATTACKS

Thank God, through the years we felt that we were being blessed. The Lord was leading us on, and we were learning. But the enemy was unhappy with us, and because of that he struck at the very center of our meeting together.

Some of the responsible brothers along with others left the assembly. As I look back, I think the reason for it was jealousy. But thank God, by His grace we continued on. However, the enemy's work was not finished yet. Again, we had another break from the center. It was over a matter of the teaching and doctrine of the Word of God. We felt there was error in some of the teaching that was coming in; but even so there were those who wanted to introduce that teaching in our midst. Because of that controversy we had the second break.

NO UNIFYING VISION

After we had gone through two breaks, we were so weakened spiritually that we began to compromise. That is my feeling. Instead of being faithful to what the Lord had entrusted to us, instead of being one with the same vision, we had become a mixed multitude. I feel that we have come into the situation found in the book of Judges. Everyone did what seemed right in his own sight with good intention, but there was no unifying vision anymore.

Brothers and sisters, I want to be very frank with you. I feel this is where we are. We are no longer a people with a unifying vision. If I should ask you what our vision is, I believe we would have a number of answers. Some will say the vision is for this, and others will say the vision is for that. And we all try to be faithful to what we consider as our vision; but there is no unifying vision.

You will remember what Solomon, the wisest of men, said in Proverbs: "Where there is no vision (singular number) the people disintegrate" (see 29:18). Or as another version says, "the people perish."

It is an absolute necessity that we have a unifying vision. We all have our own ideas, so how can we be together as one? What really brings us together as one, not just outwardly but inwardly? How?

8

The secret is in vision. Our hearts need to be together as one, as we sacrifice and lay down our own thoughts, and press on together because there is a vision that unifies us and it is worthwhile.

Thank God, He gives charges to His people. Some people may have a charge from the Lord for evangelism. Thank God for that. I remember when Billy Graham had his crusade in New York. We all went to serve as counselors even though we felt we could not join in because that organization included even modernists, who were people who did not believe in the Bible. But nevertheless, we all went to be counselors and to help.

What is the vision that began this meeting? We do not despise evangelism because this is the first step. Without evangelism there can be no discipleship, and without discipleship there can be no church testimony. But why are we here? I ask myself this question, and I want to humbly ask every brother and sister who is meeting with us to ask himself or herself the same question. We are nobody, just a small group. There is nothing to boast of. But if we have a vision, there is something worthwhile for us to continue on and even pay whatever cost there will be.

DOES THIS GATHERING MEAN SOMETHING TO THE LORD?

We do not want to be merely existing here. There is no meaning to that. If it does not mean something to the Lord, why should we be here? We want to be of value to the Lord Himself. We want to give ourselves to that vision in order that the Lord's purpose for our gathering together may be fulfilled. We are not seeking for numbers. We want to be those who have the vision that unites us into one. A people without vision merely exist, but a people with vision pay a cost. Are we willing to pay the cost? Are we willing to lay down our own preferences? Are we willing to bear the cross and follow the Lord? After forty years I think it is time for us to reflect; otherwise we are wasting our lives.

THE MISSION OF THE CHURCH

In the beginning the vision God gave us was very simple—it is the testimony of Jesus. This is the charge that God has given to the church. What is the mission of the church? The mission of the church is to bear the testimony of Jesus. The Lord said, "I will build My church upon this rock, and the gates of Hades shall not prevail against it." The Lord is building His church upon Himself, and that which He is building is an expression of what He is. And it is the charge to the church to bear the testimony of Jesus. We declare that He is Lord and that He is in charge of us. We have no opinion of our own. We want to do everything He calls us to do and nothing that He has not called us to concerning the testimony of Jesus. That is what it is.

THE WORD OF GOD AND
THE TESTIMONY OF JESUS

As you read church history, you discover how the saints throughout the ages suffered for the Word of God and for the testimony of Jesus. The apostle John was exiled for that very reason, and he told us in Revelation 1 that it was "for the Word of God and for the testimony of Jesus." But thank God, it is worth it. Our Lord Himself laid down His own life for that testimony, and we are supposed to carry on the testimony. The whole Bible is the testimony of Jesus.

When our Lord was raised from the dead, he talked with two brothers who were so disappointed at the death of Jesus that they left Jerusalem and travelled toward Emmaus. And on the way the Lord explained to them the whole Bible and how it speaks of Him. How He revealed and revived their sunken hearts! He explained the same thing to the disciples who gathered in Jerusalem by using Deuteronomy, the Law, the Psalms, and the prophets. This is the testimony of Jesus. He Himself testified, "I am the first and the last and the living one. I was dead but now I live forevermore, and I have the keys of death and Hades" (see Revelation 1:17b-18). That is the testimony. That is the vision we had from the very beginning.

THE CROSSROADS

I feel we are at a crossroads. I think it is time for us as a people to review our past and to be very honest before the Lord. Where do we want to go? Why do we meet together? What is our purpose? We do not want to waste our time anymore because the coming of the Lord is imminent. We are going to see Him very soon—sooner than we think. How are we going to answer Him?

I am exposing myself by laying this whole matter before you. I hope you do not take it lightly, but you will be serious about it. Look at our time of worship. Where are the praises and worship? I notice that people do not even sing anymore much less offer praises. We have fallen. May the Lord have mercy upon us! I think it is time for us to wake up, and not go on as usual. This is an unusual time, and I think it tests us to the uttermost. Let us be honest before the Lord. Are we willing to pay every cost and any cost? Are we willing to lay down ourselves, our own petty subjects, and allow the Lord to get through to us for the testimony of

Jesus? That is the burden of my heart. Forgive me if I am too bold, but I wanted to be honest with you.

May we have some prayer. Amen.

WHAT IS OUR VISION?

Proverbs 29:18—Where there is no vision the people cast off restraint; but happy is he that keepeth the law.

Hebrews 1:1-3—God having spoken in many parts and in many ways formerly to the fathers in the prophets, at the end of these days has spoken to us in [the person of the] Son, whom he has established heir of all things, by whom also he made the worlds; who being [the] effulgence of his glory and [the] expression of his substance, and upholding all things by the word of his power, having made [by himself] the purification of sins, set himself down on the right hand of the greatness on high.

Let's have a word of prayer:

Dear Lord, as we continue in Thy presence, we pray that Thou wilt reveal Thyself to us. Do not allow us to know Thee by hearsay, but Lord, we want to know Thee intimately because Thou art everything to us. As we gather here, Lord, we want to open ourselves to Thee and pray that Thy Spirit will reveal Christ to us in such a way that we will catch the vision and continue to live and to serve according to Thy will. We ask in Thy precious name. Amen.

WITHOUT VISION
PEOPLE CAST OFF RESTRAINT

Solomon, the wisest of men, spoke three thousand proverbs and was the one who was used by God to give us the book of Proverbs. Of course, we know in the book of Proverbs there are only three hundred and seventy-five proverbs which means we do not have all of Solomon's proverbs. However, there is one verse in Proverbs that is particularly important and that is in chapter 29:18: "Where there is no vision, the people cast off restraint."

In this verse, it is not visions (plural), but vision (singular). There is *the* vision that is absolutely important to God's people. If there is no vision, the Bible says "the people cast off restraint." We need to be restrained. Even when God created man, He gave him restraint. He told him that he could freely eat of every tree in the garden except the tree of the knowledge of good and evil. That is restraint. The reason God put restraint on man is because He knows us. We want to be free—especially in this country we do not want any restraint. We just want to be and do what we want to, and we feel that is great. But actually, man needs restraint; he needs vision. If there is no vision, people cast off restraint. In other words, people will do whatever they think is best.

CONFUSION IS A RESULT OF EVERY MAN DOING WHAT IS RIGHT IN HIS OWN EYES

That is the situation that is found in the book of Judges. After all these things that are described in the book of Judges, the Holy Spirit gave this comment in the last verse of the last chapter: "There was no king in Israel; every man

14

did what was right in his own eyes" (21:25). That describes the book of Judges—confusion. There was no restraint. Everyone went his or her own way, thinking their own way was the best. And when that is the case, there is no unity. Some versions say "people disintegrate" because each goes his or her own way. Other versions say "the people perish" because the enemy is able to divide God's people by attacking each one individually and no one is able to overcome. So this matter of God's people having *the* vision is very serious.

THE OLD TESTAMENT VISION WAS THE LAW

In the Old Testament time, God gave vision to God's people Israel, and that vision was the law. When they kept the law, the people were safe; but when they rebelled against the law, the people perished. Now that was during the Old Testament time; but we are in the New Testament time now. Law was the vision for the Old Testament people; but what is the vision for God's people today?

TODAY GOD HAS REVEALED HIMSELF IN HIS SON

In the book of Hebrews in the first chapter it says that God revealed Himself in pieces and bits through the prophets. No one prophet could give the whole vision of God; each one would give a little bit more. But in our day, He has revealed Himself in His Son. In other words, God's Son is the vision.

John 1:17 says, "The law came through Moses, grace and truth subsist in Christ Jesus." The word *subsist* in the

15

original Greek means it has never been on the earth before, but it began and is carried on by Jesus Christ. No one knows what grace is. It does not mean grace was not there because God was there; but on earth grace was not there. Grace and truth came through Jesus Christ. They were and they are in Jesus Christ. So what is the vision in our day that really unites God's people together, gives us restraint and enables us to be one instead of each going his or her own way? It is the vision of our Lord Jesus, and that is what you find in the book of Ephesians.

In Ephesians 1 it says: "Having made known to us the mystery of his will, according to his good pleasure which he purposed in himself for [the] administration of the fulness of times; to head up all things in the Christ, the things in the heavens and the things upon the earth; in him" (vv. 9-10).

CHRIST JESUS IS TO HEAD UP ALL THINGS IN THE HEAVENS AND UPON THE EARTH

In other words, the vision that God gives to us is the vision of His beloved Son, Christ Jesus, because God wants Him to head up all things in the heavens and upon the earth. In some versions it says "to sum up"—He is to sum up everything in Christ. What does it mean? In Romans there is the same expression when it speaks of the law. What is the commandment of God? We have Ten Commandments and many statutes and other things, but they can all be summed up in one thing—"love God with all your heart" (see Deuteronomy 6:5). That is summing up all the commandments of the law. In the same way, it is Christ who is to sum up all things, no matter what thing it is. It is to be an expression of Christ. Simply put, the vision that God gives to us is the vision of Christ. He is the all-inclusive vision, and it is that vision which really unites us into one.

PERSONAL TESTIMONY

What Does Serving the Lord Really Mean?

I remember after I was saved, I was so grateful to God that I wanted to serve Him but I did not know what serving Him really meant. I only knew I wanted to do something for Him because He had done so much for me. One day I volunteered to go to Mongolia to preach the gospel. That was my way of expressing my gratitude to Him. It was very serious to me. I was at that time in my senior year, and I began to prepare myself for that. I gathered all the material I could find concerning Mongolia. Not only that, I thought the only way to serve God was to go to a Bible school to study the Bible. I was active among the Christians in Shanghai so I knew all of the different denominations, their works and their Bible schools. I chose one that I thought was the best and I began to prepare to go after I finished high school. I did not want to go to college because I thought it was a waste of four years. I thought certainly my father would agree with that because he was a pastor and loved God. But unfortunately, and fortunately, my father disagreed. He said, "No, you are going to college. After you finish college, I will send you to America to study theology." I was very disappointed. All of my plans were smashed; but in China we learned to obey our parents.

So I went to college which was a Christian school. The professors were American missionaries. When I went there, I immediately got involved in all of the Christian activities. But to my great surprise I discovered my professors, who were missionaries from America, did not believe the Bible

17

as the Word of God. They talked about the Bible but only on social things and other things like that. They did not believe that Jesus is the Son of God. Whenever I tried to mention it, they cut me down. I was surprised. I did not know what was happening. I thought all Christians believed in Christ. I did not know there were Christians called modernists. After a while, I withdrew from the activities because I could not go on like that.

Seeing the Church

At that time, I lived in the dormitory with three other people in the same room. Every day I knelt by my chair, read the Bible and prayed. Schoolmates were going in and out, but I did not care because that was my lifeline. I could not live spiritually without reading the Word of God and praying. It was during that time that the Lord began to open my eyes, and the first thing I saw was the church. I was a member of the Methodist church in which I was very faithful and active. But I began to see that the church is not Methodist or Baptist or whatever name it goes by. The church is one in Christ Jesus. So when the Lord spoke to me about it, gradually I began to understand in a small way. As a pastor's son, it was difficult, especially at that time because people knew I was to succeed my father.

I struggled over this whole matter. Then the Lord brought together seven of us, two of my classmates and four sisters from a Presbyterian hospital. As we got to know each other we had the same thought. We prayed and sought the Lord about it: "What shall we do?" And by the grace of God, He brought us together.

Breaking Bread

I still remember the first time the seven of us gathered together to break the bread. We all wept because we were so moved within. Then God began to bring others in. During that time, the main responsibility was upon me. This is what I did. I was the one who opened the doors and welcomed the people, the one who lead the singing, the one who preached, the one who sent them away and closed the doors. I did everything; I was so busy. My mother began to wonder if I ever studied because when I came back late at night and tried to study I fell asleep when I was studying in bed. My mother had to come and cover me. So she was concerned. But when she saw my grades were good, she had nothing to say. During my years in college, the Lord did miracle after miracle with my school work. Now I dare not tell you what these miracles were because when I said this in other places, someone tried to imitate me and it did not work.

Traveling with Brother Nee

When I graduated, I was supposed to be employed by my school. My professor wanted me to be his assistant, but it was not to be. Brother Nee asked me to join him, so I began to work together with him. I was only twenty years old, and it was the first time I had left home. I stayed in the upper room of the gospel bookroom and there was no one over me. I could have been ruined because I had so much time on my hands. Fortunately, I like to read, and brother Nee would give me books to read every week—all kinds of books. Then I began to travel all over China from city to city holding evangelistic meetings. My work was to preach the gospel, get people saved, and after they were saved, there were four things I was to do. One: I was to get them baptized. Two: I was to gather them together to break bread and remember the Lord. Three: I was to get the sisters to cover their heads. Four: I was to get them to leave the denominations. Those were mainly the four works I did for some years until I was tired of it. Of course, we also had Bible study. I tried to lead them in how to study the Bible. But I began to think: What more can I do?

Seeing the Immensity of Christ

Thank God, when World War II began, I was in Singapore. Before Singapore fell, the Lord miraculously led me out and I went to south India where I stayed for two and a half months. During my quiet times while there, I began to read brother Sparks' books, and the Lord began to open my eyes to see Christ. I was on the verge of thinking what I could do next and the Lord opened my eyes to see the immensity of Christ. So I told the Lord: "Thank You; now I know what I am to do, and by the grace of God, that is what I have been doing until now. There is no limit to this vision.

THE OLD TESTAMENT PROPHETS RECEIVED VISION

Vision is so important. When we read the Old Testament, we find that the patriarchs and the prophets were raised up by God with vision. They all had vision or revelation they had received from God. Vision is what you see spiritually; revelation is what you hear and understand. But they are one and the same.

Noah had vision of the judgment of God and he prepared the ark for the salvation of his family. Abraham had vision, and God gave him revelation. He told him to leave his home and even his family and go to the place God would show him, and by faith he obeyed. Before Moses had vision, he tried to serve God in his own strength, and he was a failure and had to escape for his life. But when he was eighty years old, God gave him the vision. After he saw the vision, God sent him back and used him. When Isaiah went into the temple to pray, he was unsure of the future of the nation; then he saw God on the throne and knew He was in control of everything. The burden of God also came to Habakkuk. You cannot really serve God without vision.

THE CHURCH IS THE VESSEL TO CONTAIN CHRIST

Of course, for us, it is the vision of Christ, and it is all inclusive. Oftentimes we think that evangelism is our vision. It is true; but it is just the beginning of our vision, not the end. When people read the great commission in Matthew 28, it is often read like this: "Go to the nations, preach the gospel and get people saved." No, it says, "Go to the nations and disciple the nations." In other words, evangelism is just the beginning of that vision. It is not because heaven is so empty that God just wants to fill heaven with people. No, God has a purpose. He wants His Son to be expressed through a body which is the church. The church is Christ—not anything else. If there is someone else other than Christ, it is foreign particles, and it is damaging to the church. The church is to be the body or the vessel to contain Christ. The church is to be the instrument in God's hand to bring all things to the feet of Jesus. This is, I believe, what God has committed to us.

We need more than just hearing about Christ. We have heard a lot; we know a lot. But how much of Christ is really our life? How much of Christ can people see in us and not ourselves? Is He the head of the church? Is He the body of the church? Is He everything? Does our understanding and horizon of Christ grow and grow or are we becoming stagnant?

VISION WILL CONTINUE TO GROW

So vision is something that will continue to grow. It is not that you see it once and that is it. No. When we read the life of Paul, we can see that on the road to Damascus he saw the vision of Christ; but fourteen years later he was taken up to the third heaven and to Paradise. Many people believe that when Christ was resurrected and ascended, He took Paradise out of earth to heaven, but there is no Scriptural evidence for that. Paradise is still under the earth. Paul heard in Paradise things that he could not describe, so he was forbidden to speak of them. But he did not say that what he saw and heard in the third heaven was forbidden. Therefore, we do believe that the revelations we find in Ephesians and Colossians are the revelations of the third heaven. So we can see that our revelation or vision of Christ needs to be increasing all the time. If it is Christ there is no end of revelation. Even in eternity we will still continue to know more of Him. That is the thrill of it. We will not be stagnant. We will be going on by the grace of God into more and more understanding of Christ.

So the problem is how much of Christ do we really know? How much of Christ do we really experience?

TO WHOM WILL GOD REVEAL HIS SON?

We know that unless God reveals, we can never understand. But our God is a God who reveals Himself. Even in Genesis, when Hagar fled from her master, God appeared to her and she said, "Thou art the God who reveals himself" (see 16:13). What God reveals is given to us and

22

we are held responsible for it. What is hidden belongs to God.

Why is it that some of God's people seem to have more revelation than others? Why is it that some people who have believed in the Lord for many years and yet their understanding and revelation are still very limited? To whom will the Lord reveal Himself?

OUR ATTITUDE HAS MUCH TO DO WITH VISION

Of course, we know that the Sermon on the Mount says, "Blessed are the poor in spirit for theirs is the kingdom of the heavens" (Matthew 5:3). "Poor in spirit" does not mean poor spirit; it means that in the spirit, there are riches, and yet there is that sense in one's self of wanting to know more because he considers what he knows is just a little. He is not proud of what he has known or satisfied with what he has been given, but he is always with a poor spirit waiting to be filled. Are we poor in spirit?

It also says, "Blessed are those who hunger and thirst after righteousness." Are we hungry for God or do we feel satisfied, quite happy with what we have already received? If that is the case, vision and revelation will end there.

The Bible also says, "Blessed are the pure in heart, for they shall see God." Do we have an ulterior motive? Do we have our own ambition hidden behind it? Or is our heart pure towards God? Do we want Him and that is it?

The Bible also tells us: "Ask and it shall be given, seek and you shall find, knock and it shall be opened to you." Are we really asking, seeking, and knocking?

It is our attitude that has much to do with vision and revelation. If our attitude is that we are full, we know everything just like the church in Laodicea, then there will be no more revelation or vision given. But if we are really humble before the Lord, considering what we know to be just a tiny bit, we want to know more of Christ, and we really seek Him earnestly, diligently, and humbly, I believe more vision or more revelation will be given to us.

IS OUR VISION ONE?

I only have one burden and it is this: What is the vision that God has given us as a people—not just individually, but as a people. We have been meeting together for forty years, and even though people have changed, and some have come and some have gone, yet we are still here. What are we here for? I think it is time for us to reflect. We want to be open before the Lord. We want Him to examine each and every one of us as to whether our vision is one or whether we have different visions. And if we have different visions, we cannot be one. Even though outwardly we may be together, but everyone is going after his or her own vision. God have mercy upon us. Let us seek the Lord together earnestly and ask Him to give us *the* vision that will really unite us into one and enable us to be a testimony to Christ.

Let's pray:

Dear Lord, we thank Thee for gathering us these years. We do want to be one, not according to our own thinking, but according to Thy thought. We thank Thee, our Father, that it is Thy Son who is given to us as the uniting vision. Lord, do not allow us to stay put somewhere. Give us that hunger and thirst after Thyself that we may press on towards the goal. Oh dear Lord, reveal Thyself to us, break through our barriers, our own limitations and bring us into the fullness of Christ that we may be a corporate vessel of Thy testimony. We ask this in Thy name. Amen.

THE TESTIMONY OF JESUS

Revelation 1:1-2, 9, 17-18—Revelation of Jesus Christ, which God gave to him, to shew to his bondmen what must shortly take place; and he signified it , sending by his angel, to his bondman John, who testified the word of God, and the testimony of Jesus Christ, all things that he saw...I John, your brother and fellow-partaker in the tribulation and kingdom and patience, in Jesus, was in the island called Patmos, for the word of God, and for the testimony of Jesus...And when I saw him I fell at his feet as dead; and he laid his right hand upon me, saying, Fear not; I am the first and the last, and the living one: and I became dead, and behold, I am living to the ages of ages, and have the keys of death and of hades.

May we have a word of prayer:

Dear Lord, we want to thank Thee again for inviting us to Thy table. We have tasted Thy love and we have received Thy life. Lord, may we all live henceforth for Thyself. We thank Thee for gathering us together. Prepare our hearts; remove any hindrance or resistance that may be in us. Lord, we pray that Thou would by Thy Spirit speak to each and every one of us here. Do not let us go our way, but we pray that we may go Thy way and allow Thee to work out Thy full salvation to the praise of Thy glory. We ask in Thy name. Amen.

UNIFYING VISION

We have shared on vision and God's Word says, "Where there is no vision, the people disintegrate, the people scatter, the people cast off restraint, or the people perish" (see Proverbs 29:18). There is the vision that God gave to His people in the Old Testament which is the law. It was the law that joined God's people together and allowed them to be a testimony to the world. But in the New Testament *the* vision is Christ. It is that vision of Christ that truly unites God's people together. It not only unites, but it gives us restraints; otherwise, we would each go our own way which is the result of sin. We know at the very beginning after Adam and Eve sinned, God came down and inquired of Adam. He put the blame on Eve, and when God inquired of Eve, she put the blame on the serpent. In other words, without *the* vision, people disintegrate. Everyone is thinking of himself or herself. It is *the* vision that unites us into one and enables us to press on together. And of course this vision is Christ which really unites us together.

We do know that in the Bible there is vision singular and visions plural. In II Corinthians 12 Paul said, "Now I am going to talk about visions and revelations" (v. 1). Nevertheless, whatever visions there may be, they all center upon Christ. Christ Jesus is *the* vision. We must be occupied with Christ instead of other things, and that will really join us together and enable us to press on towards the goal.

THE VESSEL OF THE TESTIMONY

Now we will share on the testimony of Jesus. The testimony of Jesus is entrusted to the church which is the vessel of that testimony; that is to say, the church is to contain Christ. Everything about the church is to be Christ Himself. Christ is so incorporated into the life of God's people that everything speaks of Him.

I Corinthians 12:12 says, "For even as the body is one and has many members, but all the members of the body, being many, are one body, so also [is] the Christ.

Now, of course, to our understanding when we think of the body as being one, we know it refers to the church; yet the church has many members. Even though there are many members, it is one body. From the beginning to the very end, from the first Christian to the last Christian, there is only one body, but it contains many members. We cannot count the number because from the first century until today we do not know how many Christians have formed the body. It is an immense body but it is one. We know this speaks of the church, but strangely, the Holy Spirit ends up by saying, "so also is *the* Christ." In other words, we do not find in the body anyone other than Christ Himself.

CHRIST IS THE CHURCH

I remember a conference in the early sixties when brother Sparks, brother Fromke, and myself were the speakers. One time I wanted to use a formula, but I knew brother Sparks was dead set against formulas because he felt that when something became a formula, it was dead. So I asked his permission to use an illustration of a formula. I said: "What is the church? Is the church you, me, he or she? For instance, if we picked the three best Christians, maybe James, John, and Peter, and it was asked: "What is the church?" We may say, "John, James, and Peter equal the church." Now everyone shook their head yes. Then I said again: "What is the church? Christ in James plus Christ in

John plus Christ in Peter equals the church." Many nodded their heads and said, "That's it! That is what the church is." Now if that is the case, it is no wonder that the church is in such trouble because John, James, and Peter all wanted to be the leader. Peter wanted to be the first. Of course, the two brothers were not far behind him.

You remember how they acted when Christ was going to Jerusalem for the last time. They thought Christ was going to be crowned and this would be their last chance to secure their place in the kingdom. James and John called for their mother, who was an aunt of our Lord Jesus, humanly speaking. They got her to ask the Lord for something, and she knew what they were asking was something that could not be spoken of publically. Nevertheless, she did ask the Lord: "I want You to give me something." She did not mention what that something was. In other words, what she was saying was this: "Here is a blank check, sign it, and I will fill in what it is for." But our Lord Jesus never signs a blank check, so He asked her: "What do you really want?" And she had to say, "Let my two sons sit on Your right and Your left." Now when the other ten disciples heard about it, they were so indignant. They were angry because they thought these two brothers had gotten the upper hand. Everyone wanted to be the head, the chief. If it is Christ in John plus Christ in James plus Christ in Peter, it does not equal the church because as long as there is Peter, John and James in their natural man, there is trouble. So finally I said, "What is the church?" It is Christ in James minus James, plus Christ in John minus John, plus Christ in Peter minus Peter that equals the church. Then everyone agreed that was right.

So in the church, outwardly you may see all the people, but God does not see us; He only sees Christ in each one of

30

us. The church is *the* Christ and it is to contain nothing but Christ. The church is not supposed to be represented by any people; the church is to be represented by Christ Himself. It is *the* Christ.

THE CHURCH IS TO BEAR THE TESTIMONY OF CHRIST

And not only is the church to be the vessel of Christ, it is also to bear the testimony of Christ. From the early days until the coming of the Lord, the nature of the church is Christ and the mission of the church is to bear the testimony of Jesus.

We find in the Word of God that John was on the island of Patmos. Of the twelve apostles John was the last one still living towards the end of the first century, and he ministered to the churches in Asia Minor in his latter years. But while he was ministering there, he was exiled by the Roman Emperor Domitian to the island of Patmos, a small island in the Aegean Sea for the Word of God and the testimony of Jesus. On the Lord's day evidently he had some leisure, and probably he was sitting on a rock facing the Aegean Sea because on a clear day he could see the coastline of Asia Minor. That was where the churches were located that he ministered to before he was exiled. He must have been sitting there looking across the sea and thinking about those churches because he really had a pastor's heart. As he was meditating on them he saw a vision of the risen Lord.

THE LAMPSTAND OF GOLD

Now we know from the Scriptures that John was most familiar with the Lord Jesus while he was on earth and

31

probably the closest one to the Lord among the disciples. He laid upon the bosom of the Lord and asked Him questions. He was very close to the Lord and knew Him better than anyone else. Then he saw a vision of the Lord in heaven which was something new to him. He heard a voice and when he turned, he saw a vision of seven golden lampstands. These lampstands are interpreted to us as the churches. Every church is a golden lampstand. Of all the furniture in the tabernacle or temple the lampstand was of pure gold. There was no wood or anything else in it other than gold, and gold speaks of the nature of God. In other words, the church is made up of what is of God and nothing else—nothing of man.

So every church before God is a golden lampstand. Now a lampstand is not something for itself; it has a purpose and that is to hold the light which is Christ. This vessel that lifts up Christ is all of gold, all of God, and none of itself. It lifts up Christ as the light, and this is the testimony of Jesus. What is the church? The church is the vessel to hold the testimony of Jesus. It is not to speak of any person; it is only to speak of Christ.

JOHN SAW THE HIGH PRIEST WALKING IN THE MIDST OF THE SEVEN LAMPSTANDS

John saw Christ as the great High Priest walking in the midst of the seven golden lampstands. What is the ministry of Christ in heaven? We know that His ministry while He was on earth was as the Apostle of God, and He was sent by God with a mission to provide redemption for the world. And how He accomplished it! Before He died on the cross He said, "It is finished! It is accomplished!" But what is Christ doing in heaven?

I remember a story about an elderly lady who had asked to be baptized. At that time it was the custom of the elders to question her about her faith. One of the questions she was asked was: "What is Christ doing in heaven?" This lady thought for a while and then said, "Christ is looking down from heaven trying to find fault in me." Of course, she did not pass.

What is Christ doing in heaven? We know what He did on earth. He was our Savior; He provided redemption for us. But what is He doing in heaven? He is not sleeping there. He is as diligent as He was while on earth. He is our heavenly High Priest, and He is ministering to His church— to every one of us. We who are saved by Him, He will save to the uttermost. That is what Christ is doing in heaven.

He is also ministering to the churches on earth. He not only ministers to each one of us individually, but He is ministering to the churches corporately. He wrote individual letters to the seven churches and in each one He begins with a revelation of Himself. The full revelation of Christ is in chapter one, but in each letter He begins with a partial revelation of Himself. In other words, our Christ is so immense that one person or one church cannot contain Him. It takes all the Christians and all the churches to contain Christ. Each church has a special commitment or revelation of Christ given to it; that is to say it is the testimony of Jesus committed to this church. He is ministering to the church to see if this testimony is being maintained. Or to put it in another way: Can He find Himself in that church? Or will He find many things in that church that are not of Himself? That is the purpose for the vision in Revelation chapter 1.

THE FATHER TESTIFIES OF HIS SON

When John saw that vision, his reaction was to fall down as one dead. He who knew and had served Christ so well, when he saw the vision of Christ in heaven as a minister ministering to His church, he fell as one dead; for he realized what a poor ministry he had given to the churches.

What is the testimony of Jesus? When Christ was on earth, at His baptism the heavens opened, and a voice came from God: "This is my beloved Son in whom I have found My delight" (Matthew 3:17). Again on the Mount of Transfiguration the Father said, "Hear Him" ((Matthew 17:5b). And the third time is in John 12 where the Lord Jesus Christ said to the Father: "Glorify Thy name." And the Father answered: "I both have glorified and will glorify it again" (v. 28b). The Father testified for His Son. That is the testimony of the Father. We find that the whole Bible testifies of our Lord Jesus Christ.

THE WORD TESTIFIES OF JESUS

In John, chapter 5, the Lord Jesus said, "Ye search the Scriptures (that is the Old Testament), for ye think that in them ye have life eternal, and they it is which bear witness concerning me" (v.39). In other words, the whole Old Testament bears the testimony of Jesus. Then you will remember that Luke 24 tells us that after He was resurrected He met the two disciples leaving Jerusalem for Emmaus. They were so disappointed that Christ had been crucified. Even though they heard the women say that Christ had risen, they could not believe it. So they left Jerusalem and went to Emmaus. Our Lord Jesus walked with them and explained to them how the Old Testament bears witness of

Him. As the Lord opened the Scriptures to them, it says that their hearts were warmed by the Word; they were so touched. Then He appeared to the disciples who were shut in a house because of fear and explained to them from Moses' five books, the Prophets and the Psalms that they were written of Him. So the Bible is the testimony of Jesus. As we read the Bible, we see Jesus.

THE LORD JESUS TESTIFIES OF HIMSELF

Our Lord Jesus testified of Himself in Revelation 1:17b-18: "Fear not; I am the first and the last, and the living one: and I became dead, and behold, I am living to the ages of ages, and have the keys of death and of hades."

This refers to His divinity. He is God. "I am the first and the last, and the living one." When He said, "I am the first," what does it mean to us? Is He the first in our life? "I am the last." What does that mean? Is He the last to us? Is He the goal that we run after? He is the living one. Is He our life? Is He all to us?

"I became dead." That speaks of His humanity when He came to this world and died in our stead. "Behold, I am living to the ages of ages." That is His resurrection; He lives forever. "And have the keys of death and of hades." He has overcome and now has the keys.

This is what Christ is to us. This is the testimony of Jesus to us. What do we testify? We testify that He is the first and He is the last, He is the living one. He has died, but behold He is living forever and has the keys of death and of hades. That is our testimony.

Let's put it very briefly: what is the testimony of Jesus? It testifies to us that He is God and He is Man. He is our

God, He is our Savior, He is our life, He is our victory. In other words, that is the testimony that the church bears. This is the testimony of Jesus.

WHEN THE CHURCH BEARS THE TESTIMONY OF JESUS IT IS CONTESTED

Because the church is bearing the testimony of Jesus, therefore it is severely contested by God's enemy. You find there is a contest, as it were, between God and Satan, and the church is the target of it; it is in the middle. The church, of course, stands for Christ. That is the reason why the church is persecuted.

John was exiled to the island of Patmos for the Word of God and the testimony of Jesus. Throughout the centuries, we find in the history of the church how it has been persecuted and contested by the enemy of God. During the second and third centuries, the Roman Empire persecuted the church ten times; but thank God, it was because of the persecution that the church was revived.

You may have heard of the stories written by Fox about the martyrs during the second and third centuries. During the second century, Polycarp was the bishop of Smyrna. He was an old man faithful to the Lord. Through the advice of some brothers and sisters, he went to a village to avoid the attack of the Roman Empire, but he was discovered by the Roman soldiers. When they came to take him, he opened the door and invited them in. He even prepared a table for them to eat and asked permission for an hour that he might pray. He went to his room and prayed for two hours. After he finished praying, he allowed the soldiers to take him. When they brought him to the proconsul, knowing that Polycarp was an old man he tried to persuade him and said,

36

"Just burn incense to Caesar and you will be free." Polycarp said, "I have served the Lord eighty-six years, and He has been good to me. How can I deny Him?" They put him to the stake to be burned, but when they set the fire, strangely it did not touch him. Finally, a soldier thrust his spear in him and he died.

You may have also heard of a young sister in the third century who had a baby. She had trusted the Lord but she had not been baptized. She was taken into prison, and while there she was baptized. Her elderly father begged her to deny the Lord. But she stood firmly and finally was killed by animals, the spear and sword of the gladiators.

Such things have happened all over the world throughout the centuries. Even in my time it happened in China. One day over a thousand brothers and sisters all over China were taken into custody. My fellow workers and elders in Shanghai where I was living were taken and put in a meeting hall. You can see the subtlety of the enemy. They told them, "You will be released if you say that Watchman Nee has faults." Now who does not have faults? Of course our brother had faults just as we have. But they used this to divide God's people. Once you say so and so has faults your faith begins to waver. One of my fellow workers, who was also an elder there and a medical doctor, was physically weak. His family came and begged him, "Say that Watchman Nee has faults. That is true. You are not lying. Why do you not say it and then you can come home?" He said, "I know Watchman Nee has faults, but God has not asked me to say it." He refused and was put in prison. Very soon, he died.

Our brother Watchman Nee was put in prison for twenty years. He was sentenced to fifteen years but because he would not deny his faith, five more years were added. He was in a labor camp, and after the twenty years were up, he was supposed to be set free, but he died for his faith.

There is a conflict going on in this world between God and Satan, and the church is the target. But thank God, often times, God uses persecution to revive His church. More and more in this country we have begun to realize that if we want to be true to the Lord, it is difficult and we have to suffer for it. But thank God, many times it is through persecution that the church is revived.

THE CHURCH IS PURIFIED THROUGH PERSECUTION

In the past many have borne witness to the testimony of Jesus, and because of their faithfulness in witnessing, they suffered for their testimony. Now we are living towards the end of this age, and we need to be prepared for it. It seems strange that the church needs persecution to be purified. Why can it not be purified without persecution? I want to ask myself and you brothers and sisters this question: Where are we with regards to the testimony of Jesus? If we are faithful we will be persecuted; but if we are not faithful, no wonder the world will welcome us.

A. J. GORDON'S DREAM OF JESUS VISITING HIS CHURCH

Finally, I would like to tell you a story about A. J. Gordon and a dream that he had. He was a great servant of the Lord in the New England region of the United States. He was a little before my time. Actually, when brother Sparks came to this country, one of the people he wanted to visit was A. J. Gordon who was a pastor of a big church in

Boston. One day he dreamed a dream and he saw the church in session. He was sitting on the platform waiting to preach. The place was almost filled, and then he saw the usher bring in a man and seat him at the front. Somehow his attention was attracted to that man; so while he was preaching, his eyes were continually upon him. He was wondering: Who is that man? Will he approve of my preaching? What does he think about our pipe organ? What will he think about our choir? Before he finished preaching, he decided he had to see this man. It is the custom for the pastor after he finished preaching to go to the door and greet people who were leaving. After he finished preaching, he tried to get to the door as fast as he could, but the man was already gone. He asked the usher, "Who is that man?" The usher said, "Do you not know him? He is Jesus." And do you know what happened? The pipe organ was gone, the choir was gone, and everything began to change. He was used greatly by the Lord.

IS JESUS IN THE MIDST OF OUR GATHERING?

Jesus should be here in our gathering. If He is not here, woe to us. If He is here this morning, what will happen to us? Can we continue in the same way? Will there be a great change in our life and our life together? This is not a supposition. When we gather around the table to remember the Lord, do you think that the Lord is not here? If He is here, can we come to the Lord's table in the way we are doing today? What will He think of us? I believe there would be a great change. This is spiritual reality; this is not a supposition; the Lord is supposed to be here. If He is not here, why do we gather? We come here to worship Him, to express our appreciation to Him, to honor Him, to exalt Him. We do not gather together for our own sake. It is not a

39

social gathering; it is a fellowship. So I believe there is much we need to think about. The Lord is coming soon. We do not know how many more times we will have to come together. Let us be real before Him.

Shall we pray:

Dear Lord, we praise and thank Thee because Thou art real; Thy testimony is real. It is Thy pleasure to be with Thy people. It is Thy pleasure to see that Thy people reflect Thee and nothing else. Oh Lord, make it so. We commit ourselves to Thee and cry to Thee that the testimony of Jesus may be maintained here in Richmond for Your glory. Amen.

HOW WILL THE CHURCH BE MADE RIGHT?

Revelation 2:7—He that has an ear, let him hear what the Spirit says to the assemblies. (This is repeated seven times in chapters 2 and 3.) To him that overcomes, I will give to him to eat of the tree of life which is in the paradise of God.

Revelation 12:11—And 'they' have overcome him by reason of the blood of the Lamb, and by reason of the word of their testimony, and have not loved their life even unto death.

Shall we pray:

Dear Lord, as we continue in Thy presence, we want to open our hearts to Thee and say, "Lord, hast Thou anything to say to us? Speak, Thy servants heareth." In Thy Name. Amen.

The Church is to be Presented to Christ as His Bride

Once brother Sparks asked brother Nee a question: "What is the hardest thing in the Bible to be fulfilled?" And to this our brother Nee answered with Ephesians 5:27: "That 'he' might present the assembly to himself glorious, having no spot, or wrinkle, or any of such things; but that it might be holy and blameless."

To our brother this would be the hardest thing to be fulfilled—that the church shall be presented to the Lord glorious, having no spot, or wrinkle, or any of such things, holy and blameless. As we look at the church today, as we look at ourselves, as we look around us, the more we think of what the church should be, the more we begin to realize it seems more and more impossible. The church has a wonderful past, but today as we look around, as we look at ourselves, it gives us this impression: How can God's church ever be presented to Christ as His bride holy, blameless, without spot or wrinkle or any of such thought? Humanly speaking, it looks impossible; but with God nothing is impossible. He who has promised will also fulfill it. But how?

THE DIFFERENCE BETWEEN THE SEVEN LETTERS OF PAUL AND THE SEVEN LETTERS OF JOHN

We know that the apostle Paul was used by God to write seven letters to seven churches. Likewise the apostle John was used by God to write seven letters to seven churches. In comparing these seven churches, we find that when Paul wrote letters to these seven churches, in spite of the fact there were many problems, even errors in some of the churches, yet the churches were considered at that time as normal. For instance, in Philippians he mentioned elders and deacons. So the churches at that time were considered to be normal even though there were problems. So as I often say, problems can be blessings if they are solved rightly.

But when we look at the seven letters written through John, there is no mention of elders or deacons. They only speak of the angel in each church. Now we know there are two kinds of angels—the heavenly and the earthly. However, we cannot think of our Lord Jesus writing to the heavenly angel about the church on earth. So the angel here must represent an earthly messenger; but we believe it is a collective term. Since there is no more mention of elders or of deacons the order in the church seems to have been lost. Those who are spiritually responsible are to care for the spiritual condition of each church. There is a vast difference between these two sets of churches.

GOD HAS A STRATEGY TO FULFILL HIS PURPOSE

In the letters to the seven churches in Asia Minor, each one ends with a call, and the call is personal: "He that has an ear, let him hear what the Spirit says to the churches." In other words, we find that God has a strategy to complete His promise and that is the overcomers. When the mass or the majority of the people seem to have failed spiritually, God will yet raise up some overcomers, minorities, a few people who are still faithful to the Lord and maintain the testimony of Jesus in their time.

THE OLD TESTAMENT PRINCIPLE OF THE REMNANT

As a matter of fact, this strategy of God is not new at all because in the Old Testament the same principle applied even though it was called by a different name. Instead of overcomers, it was called "a remnant." The children of Israel were called by God to bear the testimony of God; but how they failed! They were taken captive to Babylon, Jerusalem was destroyed, the temple was destroyed, and there was no more testimony of God on earth. And in Daniel we find that God was called the God of the heavens and no longer called the God of the heavens and the earth because He had no testimony upon this earth. Israel had failed God.

But thank God, after seventy years of captivity in Babylon, God stirred up the hearts of a remnant. Unfortunately, the majority of the Jews in captivity remained in Babylon. During those seventy years, they were well-treated. They were able to build their own houses and their own businesses. They were well-to-do in the land of captivity; therefore, they had no desire to leave and go back to Jerusalem, which was in ruin, and rebuild the temple in order for the testimony of God to be on earth. They had no desire for that. They lived for themselves and were quite content. But thank God, the spirits of a remnant, which were comparatively few, were stirred by God. They were willing to go back to the ruined land of Jerusalem for one purpose and that was to rebuild the temple, the house of God, in order that God might have a testimony upon earth. This was the remnant principle. And when you come to the New Testament, it is the overcomer principle; but actually they are the same.

THE OVERCOMERS AT THE END OF THE FIRST CENTURY

We are now living at the very end of this age. This age of grace began at the first coming of our Lord Jesus, but it will end at the second coming of our Lord Jesus. For at His second coming He will bring in the millennial kingdom which is the thousand years that He will reign upon this earth. We are living towards the end of this age. But thank God, throughout the ages, He has His overcomers. For instance, in Revelation, chapters 2 and 3, these churches existed towards the end of the first century, but only two of these seven churches were without any blame, and the Lord called the other five to repent. But even though the church in Philadelphia seemed to be an overcoming church, yet the Lord still said, "Be faithful to the end, less you lose your crown." In other words, they were overcoming as a church, yet it was still possible that some could lose their crown. So in a sense to be an overcomer is very individual. In other words, individually we have to be responsible to be either an overcomer or to be overcome. So among all these churches in Revelation 2 and 3, whatever their conditions may have been, thank God, there were overcomers, which simply means they were faithful to the vision that God had given to them. So Revelation 2 and 3 tell us of the overcomers at the end of the first century.

THE OVERCOMERS
THROUGHOUT THE CENTURIES

But then we turn to Revelation 7:9: "After these things I saw, and lo, a great crowd, which no one could number, out of every nation and tribes and peoples and tongues, standing before the throne, and before the Lamb, clothed with white robes, and palm branches in their hands."

These are the overcomers throughout the centuries. We are now in the twenty-first century, but these represent the overcomers through the centuries from the second to the twentieth century. Therefore, even though we always think of overcomers as a minority, yet we find here a number that cannot be counted. In other words, throughout the centuries, no matter what the general condition of the church may have been, thank God there will be those who are faithful to God. So there are overcomers throughout the ages.

Revelation 7:10: "And they cry with a loud voice, saying, Salvation to our God who sits upon the throne, and to the Lamb."

Revelation 7:14: "And he said to me, These are they who come out of the great tribulation, and have washed their robes, and have made them white in the blood of the Lamb."

Now the great tribulation here is a general term. It is not the great tribulation of three and a half years because throughout the centuries, the church has been going through great tribulation. Why? The church is supposed to be the instrument of God; therefore, they have become the target of the enemy of God. And throughout the centuries, the enemy has used every means to destroy the testimony of the church. Sometimes he has used persecutions; other times he has used favor. Whether it is favor or persecution, behind it is the tactic of the enemy trying to destroy the church which is the bearer of the testimony of God, of Jesus. But thank God, throughout the centuries there have been overcomers. They came out of the tribulations, washed their robes, and made them white in the blood of the Lamb.

THE VISION OF THE WOMAN WHO BEARS THE MAN CHILD

In chapter 12 of Revelation there is a vision. "And a great sign was seen in the heaven: a woman clothed with the sun, and the moon under her feet, and upon her head a crown of twelve stars; and being with child she cried, *being in travail*, and in pain to bring forth" (12:1-2).

This is a vision of the end time. Here we see a woman who represents the church at the end time. The church is clothed with the sun; that is, it belongs to God. The moon was under her feet; that is the law under her feet. She is crowned with twelve stars which refers to the patriarch age. That is the church of the ages. And she was in travail to bring forth a man child which is the situation of the church at the end time.

THE VISION OF THE DRAGON

Then in Revelation 12:3-4a there is a vision of a dragon: "And another sign was seen in the heaven: and behold, a great red dragon, having seven heads and ten horns, and on his heads seven diadems; and his tail draws the third part of the stars of the heaven; and he cast them to the earth." That dragon represents Satan and how he drew a third of the angels to rebel against God.

"And the dragon stood before the woman who was about to bring forth, in order that when she brought forth he might devour her child" (Revelation 12:4b).

Strangely, you find the dragon is not interested in the woman, for in a sense, the woman is already in his hand. She had lost the testimony; but he was interested in the womb. The woman was in travail, and that is the wisdom of God. Even when God allowed the church to go through sufferings, tribulations, and in travail, it is to bring forth a man child. Therefore, at the end of this age, there will still be persecutions. But the object of the dragon was not the woman anymore; it was the man child. Now, of course, there are various interpretations, but we feel this is the right interpretation.

47

Some people think the man child is Christ and that the enemy was trying to swallow Him when He was born. But we all know that God protected Him. But strangely, we find that when the man child was born, he did not live on earth. Immediately after he was born, he was raptured to the third heaven to the throne. Now that is not what happened to Christ, for our Lord Jesus spent thirty-three years on earth.

THE MAN CHILD REPRESENTS THE OVERCOMERS AT THE END OF THIS AGE

Most likely this man child represents the overcomers at the end of this age before the second coming of the Lord. Satan knew that if this man child was born, it would be the end of Satan. So that is why he was so interested in devouring the man child as soon as he was born. But thank God, when the man child was born, immediately he was raptured to the throne, to God (see Revelation 12:5b).

As we read verses 10 and 11 we find that this man child actually is a collective term. It is not just one person because the Bible uses the word *they*. "They have overcome." This man child represents the overcomers at the second coming of the Lord.

Immediately after this man child was raptured to the throne, there was war in the air. It is as if this man child or the overcomers at the end of this age will be the welcoming party for the second coming of the Lord. We know that the headquarters of Satan is in the air, but this man child is able to thrust through the air to reach the throne, and that seems to speak of overcoming. They have overcome Satan in their lives, and because of that, they are raptured to the throne.

THE RAPTURE OF THE OVERCOMERS

This brings us to what our Lord Jesus said in Matthew 24, that at His coming something will happen. "Two women will be grinding; one is taken and one is left (v. 41). Two will be working in the fields; one is taken and one is left (v. 40). Two will be sleeping; one will be taken and one is left" (see Luke 17:34). What does it mean? What will be the sign of the Lord's coming? At the second coming of the Lord, suddenly all over this world some Christians will disappear. It is not six people. The "two" represents the Christians who are living at the time of the coming of the Lord. It speaks of us because we are living towards the end of this age. Why is it two and not twelve, because we know that twelve is the number of the church, which is a complete number? If we look in chapter Matthew 25 we find ten virgins which speak of Christians who have died through the ages. The two we have just referred to represent Christians who are still living at the coming of the Lord. Why does the Bible use all of these different illustrations? It is because the earth is round. In some places it is morning, at the same time in other places it is noontime, and at the same time in other places it is night so two are sleeping.

The thing we want to see is this: the Bible does not tell us any difference between the two. Outwardly they look the same. They are grinding, working in the fields, even sleeping. But the Lord knows the ones who are His. The Lord knows those who are waiting for Him. The Lord knows those who are praying and watching and waiting, prepared for His return. The Lord knows. We look at the outward appearances, and they are the same; but the Lord knows what is inside. Therefore, when the call comes, only those who can respond to the Lord will be raptured. But

49

those who do not respond to the Lord will be left behind for the Great Tribulation.

This is the promise that was given to the church in Philadelphia, that before the time of the Great Tribulation which shall come to the whole world, they will be raptured out of the world to the throne. These people who are raptured because they have overcome can thrust through the headquarters of Satan and reach the throne to be the welcoming party of the coming of the Lord.

WAR IN THE AIR

As soon as they are raptured, we are told in Revelation, chapter 12, that there will be war in the air. Michael and his angels will fight with Satan and his angels, and the result is that Satan and his angels will be thrown upon the earth and the air will be cleared. Why is it necessary for the air to be cleared? Because our Lord Jesus will descend from the throne with the overcomers to the air.

That is the reason those Christians who are not prepared, who are not ready, who are overcome instead of overcoming, will have to go through the Great Tribulation. But remember, even when they go through the Great Tribulation, it is the mercy of God because God gives them another chance. The Great Tribulation should wake up those who were not prepared for the rapture. There will be overcomers coming out of the Great Tribulation, and they shall reign with Christ.

OVERCOMERS OUT OF THE GREAT TRIBULATION

We will find this in chapter 15 where John saw another sign: "And I saw another sign in the heaven, great and wonderful: seven angels having seven plagues, the last; for in them the fury of God is completed. And I saw as a glass sea, mingled with fire, and those that had gained the victory over the beast, and over its image, and over the number of its name, standing upon the glass sea, having harps of God" (vv. 1-2).

These are overcomers who have come out of the Great Tribulation. In other words, you see the mercy of God. He has given us chance after chance, because His heart is for us to be overcomers and not to be overcome. So these will be the overcomers during the Great Tribulation that we find in chapter 15.

THE TWO MARRIAGES OF THE LAMB

The First Marriage

In chapter 19 there is the marriage feast of the Lamb; His wife has made herself ready. Strangely, we find when we read the Bible, it not only begins with a marriage as found in Genesis 2, but the Bible ends with a marriage. But then towards the end of the book of Revelation, we discover that there are two marriages of the Lamb—one in chapter 19 and one in chapter 21 and 22.

"And I heard as a voice of a great crowd, and as a voice of many waters, and as a voice of strong thunders, saying, Hallelujah, for [the] Lord our God the Almighty has taken to himself kingly power. Let us rejoice and exult, and give

51

him glory; for the marriage of the Lamb is come, and his wife has made herself ready. And it was given to her that she should be clothed in fine linen, bright [and] pure; for the fine linen is the righteousnesses of the saints" (Revelation 19:6-8). This is the first marriage mentioned.

The Second Marriage of the Lamb

"And I saw a new heaven and a new earth; And I saw the holy city, new Jerusalem, coming down out of the heaven from God, prepared as a bride adorned for her husband" (Revelation 21:1a, 2). This is the second marriage.

Why are there two marriages? What is the difference? Are they the same? If you read carefully you will find that these two marriages are a thousand years apart. Chapter 19 is the marriage of the Lamb at the beginning of the millennium. In chapters 21 and 22 is the marriage of the Lamb when the thousand years are over and eternity begins. So as we read these chapters carefully, we will find there is a difference between the two marriages.

The Wedding Garment

In chapter 19 the bride is not represented by the whole church; she is represented only by the overcomers of the ages. How do we know this? It is described in verse 8: "[They are] clothed in fine linen, bright [and] pure; for the fine linen is the righteousnesses of the saints." In other words, all who believe in the Lord Jesus are clothed with Christ who is our righteousness, and that clothing gives us standing before God. But over and above that clothing, there will be another garment—a wedding garment. The wedding garment is the righteousnesses of the saints. The basic clothing of a Christian is the righteousness of Christ—Christ our righteousness. But the wedding garment is the righteousnesses of the saints. In other words, after we are clothed with Christ, in our daily life we should be allowing the life of Christ to live in and through us, and out of that comes the righteousnesses of the saints. In Psalm 45 we see that the bride, the queen, is clothed with two garments: the golden one and the linen one. The golden one represents Christ our righteousness. The linen one represents what the Holy Spirit has worked in our lives, stich by stitch, until it becomes a wedding garment. Do we have the righteousnesses of the saints? Is the righteousness of Christ being lived out through us?

In chapter 19 of Revelation this wedding begins the millennium. We do not know how long this wedding goes on; maybe a thousand years. And in Matthew 25 we discover why the five foolish virgins could not enter into the marriage feast; they were in darkness.

However, God can never fail. We may fail but God will never fail. Once He has saved us, He will save us to the uttermost. That is what Paul says in Romans 8: "Whom He has foreordained, He has called; whom He has called, He has justified; whom He has justified, He has glorified" (v. 30). In other words, when God's hand comes upon you, thank God, it is always towards perfection. He will never leave anything undone. If you cooperate, it is sooner. If you do not cooperate, sooner or later, you will by His grace be perfected. However, during the millennium time, you may be in darkness; that is discipline. If you do not allow the discipline today, in the millennium time you will be disciplined because He wants you to be like Him.

THE CONSUMMATION OF ALL THE WORK OF GOD THROUGHOUT THE AGES

When we come to Revelation 21 and 22 we will find that it is the consummation of all the marvelous work of God—both from the Old Testament and the New Testament time. The foundation is the twelve apostles which is the New Testament, but the gates are the names of the twelve tribes of Israel. In other words, it is the consummation of all the work of God. Everyone will be a king who sees the face of our Lord constantly.

Now that is in the future. How about today? We are still living, but we are on the verge of that rapture. Are we prepared? Are we ready? No one knows who is ready. Only God knows. But how can we be ready? How can we live an overcoming life?

The secret is in Revelation 12:11: "And 'they' have overcome him by reason of the blood of the Lamb, and by reason of the word of their testimony, and have not loved their life even unto death." How can we overcome Satan in our lives?

THE SECRET OF BEING READY FOR THE RAPTURE

By the Blood of the Lamb

Do not think that we need the blood of the Lamb only when we are saved. It is the blood of the Lamb that has saved us, but here we find that the blood of the Lamb is needed throughout our lifetime. How we need His blood every day, every moment. The closer we are with the Lord, the more we realize how much we need the blood. Even the tears of our repentance need His blood. We will never come to a time when we will not need the blood of the Lamb. No one is perfect; we all have our failures and imperfections. But the Holy Spirit is working in us to conform us to be like the Lord Jesus. The only way through is by the blood of the Lamb. We need His cleansing all the time.

By the Word of Their Testimony

They have a testimony. What is the testimony? It is the testimony of Jesus. In other words, they can bear the testimony of Jesus, and they can speak the word of the testimony. They can speak the word "Jesus is Lord". And when they speak that word, it is powerful. It works; it defeats the enemy.

You will remember the story in Acts 19 when Paul was in Ephesus. There were seven sons of the Jewish high priest Sceva, who were exorcists, and they tried to drive demons out of people. But when they saw Paul was successful in praying in the name of the Lord Jesus and the demons were driven out, two of them tried to use that formula. They thought it was a formula. They said, "By Jesus of whom Paul has preached we command you demons to leave." However, the demons said, "Jesus I know, Paul I am acquainted with, but who are you?" And the demons overcame two of them, and they fled naked and wounded. The word of the testimony is real. Of course, if you do not have the reality behind it, it does not work, but if you have the reality behind it, it works. The demons will be driven out by the word of the testimony.

John the apostle had the testimony of Jesus. Even though he had to be exiled, he had the testimony of Jesus. Do we have the testimony of Jesus? When we say Jesus is

Lord, is He really Lord of our life or are we still our own lord?

They Loved Not Their Lives Even Unto Death

The life here is soul-life. In other words, they are willing to lay down their soul-life to follow the Lord. The Lord said, "If you love your soul-life, you will lose it. If you lose it for My sake, you will gain it to eternity." That is the salvation of the soul. Do we have such a spirit before the Lord? Are we willing to lay down ourselves and allow the Lord to be really Lord over us?

These are the secrets of the overcomers. They are open secrets. They are for every one of us, and we all can become overcomers by the grace of God.

Are we ready? If tonight, the call comes, will we go? May the Lord help us!

Shall we pray:

Dear Lord, how we praise and thank Thee that Thou art still waiting. Thou art still patiently waiting for us. Lord, do not allow us to miss the opportunity. Do touch our hearts, enable us to really give ourselves totally to Thee and allow Thee to have full authority over our lives. Make us ready and use us as those who prepare for Thy imminent return. We commit one another into Thy hand. None of us can boast of ourselves but we all humbly put ourselves into Thy hand and pray that none of us will miss the opportunity. We ask in Thy name. Amen.

Other Books Printed By
Christian Testimony Ministry

SPEAKER	TITLE
DANA CONGDON	MARRIAGE, SINGLENESS, AND THE WILL OF GOD
	RECOVERY & RESTORATION
	THE HOLY SPIRIT
	HEBREWS
A.J. FLACK	TENT OF HIS SPLENDOUR
	ACTS
STEPHEN KAUNG	BE YE THEREFORE PERFECT
	CALLED OUT UNTO CHRIST
	CALLED TO THE FELLOWSHIP OF GOD'S SON
	DIVINE LIFE AND ORDER
	FOR ME TO LIVE IS CHRIST
	GLORIOUS LIBERTY OF THE CHILDREN OF GOD
	GOD'S PURPOSE FOR THE FAMILY
	I WILL BUILD MY CHURCH
	MEDITATIONS ON THE KINGDOM
	RECOVERY
	SPIRITUAL EXERCISE
	SPIRITUAL LIFE (II CORINTHIANS SERIES)
	TEACH US TO PRAY
	THE CROSS
	THE FULNESS OF CHRIST—IN THE BOOK OF REVELATION
	THE HEADSHIP OF CHRIST
	THE KINGDOM AND THE CHURCH
	THE KINGDOM OF GOD
	THE LAST CALL TO THE CHURCHES, THE CALL TO OVERCOME
	THE LIFE OF OUR LORD JESUS
	THE LIFE OF THE CHURCH, THE BODY OF CHRIST
	THE LORD'S TABLE
	TWO GUIDEPOSTS FOR INHERITING THE KINGDOM
	VISION OF CHRIST (REVELATION)
	WHO ARE WE?
	WHY DO WE SO GATHER?
	WORSHIP

LANCE LAMBERT   CALLED UNTO HIS ETERNAL GLORY
                        GOD'S ETERNAL PURPOSE
                        IN THE DAY OF THY POWER
                        JACOB I HAVE LOVED
                        LIVING FAITH
                        LESSONS FROM THE LIFE OF MOSES
                        LOVE DIVINE
                        MY HOUSE SHALL BE A HOUSE OF PRAYER
                        PREPARATION FOR THE COMING OF THE LORD
                        REIGNING WITH CHRIST
                        SPIRITUAL CHARACTER
                        THE GOSPEL OF THE KINGDOM
                        THE IMPORTANCE OF COVERING
                        THE LAST DAYS AND GOD'S PRIORITIES
                        THE PRIZE
                        THE SUPREMACY OF JESUS CHRIST
                        THINE IS THE POWER!
                        THOU ART MINE

T. AUSTIN-SPARKS   THE LORD'S TESTIMONY AND THE WORLD NEED

HARVEY CEDARS CONFERENCE

STEPHEN KAUNG   HEAVENLY VISION
                        SPIRITUAL RESPONSIBILITY

CONGDON, HILE, KAUNG   SPIRITUAL MINISTRY
                        SPIRITUAL AUTHORITY
                        SPIRITUAL HOUSE
                        SPIRITUAL SUBMISSION

STEPHEN KAUNG   SPIRITUAL VALUE
                        SPIRITUAL DISCERNMENT
                        SPIRITUAL BLESSING
                        SPIRITUAL WARFARE
                        SPIRITUAL ASCENDANCY
                        SPIRITUAL KNOWLEDGE
                        SPIRITUAL POWER
                        SPIRITUAL REALITY
                        SPIRITUAL MINDEDNESS

SPIRITUAL PERFECTION
SPIRITUAL FULNESS
SPIRITUAL SONSHIP
SPIRITUAL STEWARDSHIP
SPIRITUAL TRAVAIL
SPIRITUAL INHERITANCE
HARVEY CEDARS CONFERENCE:
HILE, KAUNG, LAMBERT
THE KING IS COMING